Original title:
Maple Memoirs

Copyright © 2025 Creative Arts Management OÜ
All rights reserved.

Author: Evan Hawthorne
ISBN HARDBACK: 978-1-80567-349-1
ISBN PAPERBACK: 978-1-80567-648-5

A Chronicle of Shimmering Trails

Upon the hill where trees dance bright,
Squirrels prance in pure delight.
Jumping high, they strike a pose,
Chasing leaves like playful prose.

Beneath the boughs, we share a laugh,
Picking up the brightest half.
A tumble here, a fumble there,
Nature's jest fills up the air.

Falling leaves, a waltz of gold,
A story waiting to be told.
Where every gust plays peek-a-boo,
And whispers secrets just for you.

With acorns rolling, a game of catch,
Who knew that fun could be this thatch?
The tree trunks giggle in the sun,
As we skip around, oh what fun!

Harvesting Ashen Memories

In the chill of autumn's breeze,
We stumble through a sea of leaves.
A jacket zipper gone astray,
The wind laughs in its own way.

Gathering shadows, we make a pile,
Falling in, oh what a style!
Caught in chaos, but feeling bold,
Our laughter rings, a joy to hold.

Sipping cider, sweet as cream,
Doughnuts hanging like a dream.
One bites down, a splatter flies,
Joyful antics light our eyes.

So come and join this merry band,
Where mischief thrives and fun is planned.
With every slip and every cheer,
We lay to rest the autumn fear.

Whispers through Tree Branches

Leaves giggle in the breeze,
Secrets tangled in the trees.
Squirrels plot their next big heist,
While birds are busy casting dice.

Raccoons wear their masks with pride,
Debating if they should collide.
Branches sway with tales of old,
As acorns fall and stories unfold.

The Legacy of Autumn's Glow

Pumpkins sport their silly hats,
While critters scamper, quick as rats.
A crispness hangs in the air,
As laughter echoes everywhere.

Old leaves dance like jesters bold,
Recalling secrets never told.
Nature's paintbrush strokes with glee,
Turns the world a jolly spree.

Swaying in the Season's Breath

Chasing shadows, leaves take flight,
In this grand and leafy rite.
With every rustle, whispers cheer,
As autumn's jesters gather near.

Wind flows in with silly grace,
Tickling branches in its race.
Nature laughs, a merry sound,
As joy and mischief spin around.

Secrets Held in Bark

Bark holds tales of mischief done,
Squirrels sneaking, having fun.
Hidden treasures often found,
Among the roots beneath the ground.

A tree once gave a secret spree,
Of how it dated a bumblebee.
Laughter echoes through the glen,
As nature chuckles once again.

An Ode to Leafy Abandon

I tripped on a pile, my ego in tow,
A rustle of laughter from leaves down below.
They danced all around, in their bright, crunchy hue,
As I flailed in my fall, like a deer in a shoe.

With each playful gust, they wafted and spun,
A carpet of colors, who could have such fun?
They giggled and teased, as I waddled away,
Swearing next time I'd wear shoes made of clay.

Heartbeats Under a Leafy Arch

Under canopies grand, where heartbeats collide,
Two squirrels played tag, with no both to decide.
They chased 'round the trunks, in a nutty ballet,
While I stood astonished, just watching their play.

One squirrel took flight on a branch that was weak,
And gracefully landed—a spectacle peak!
With a flick and a flash, he waved me to cheer,
As I clapped my hands, feeling both joy and fear.

Fireside Reflections

Crackling the logs with a soft, smoky turn,
I pondered on leaves, as the embers all burn.
Did they whisper sweet tales of a time lost in flight?
Or chuckle at humans, who don't dance at night?

A tea kettle sings with a whistling voice,
While old leaves outside laugh, oh what a choice!
I sip and I ponder, with a grin on my face,
As the leaves make a ruckus, and my thoughts drift to space.

Chronicles of November's Crisp

In a garden of gold, mischief raised its head,
With a gust from the east, my hat flew instead!
It sailed like a plane, oh where could it land?
As I chased after dreams that were out of my hand.

Daffy ducks quacked at my comical plight,
As squirrels rolled in acorns, with sheer delight.
I paused to take notes, what a time, oh so grand,
In the chronicles of crisp that no one had planned.

When Leaves Speak

When leaves gather round, they gossip and giggle,
They hear secrets of squirrels and dance like a wiggle.
"Did you see that jump?" they chime with delight,
As acorns roll by, they cackle 'til night.

"Who knew the wind could tickle so sweet?"
"And who's that squirrel with the fancy new feet?"
They chuckle and flutter, carefree in air,
With chatter so silly, it's quite the affair.

Time's Ephemeral Canvas

Time paints the trees in colors so bright,
Each season a stroke, a whimsical sight.
Yet every fall, they tumble in cheer,
Saying, "Catch us if you can, we're outta here!"

In a swirl of shades, they twist and they spin,
"Have you seen our old friends? They've blown in the wind!"
As nature plays tricks on the eyes of the blind,
Leaves share funny tales while the branches unwind.

The Palette of Change

Once we were green, all fresh and pristine,
Now we sport orange, a vibrant routine.
"What's next, oh tree?" we giggle with glee,
"Will you dress us in plaid, or a polka dot spree?"

Unruly they flutter, in mischief they play,
Bidding farewell as they twirl on their way.
"Catch us if you can!" they tease with a shout,
As children below laugh and jump all about.

Whispering Woods

In the woods the trees whisper secrets of fun,
They share tales of critters who scampered and run.
"Did you hear that raccoon?" they chuckle and sway,
"He tried to steal snacks, but they slipped away!"

Every rustle a giggle, in leaves green and gold,
As they murmur of legends, both funny and bold.
The forest laughs louder, as shadows embrace,
Creating a world where humor's the grace.

Golden Hour Reflections

Leaves of gold fall from above,
Tickling noses, oh what fun!
Squirrels dance with nuts in paws,
Chasing shadows, on the run.

Sunlight giggles through the trees,
Whispers secrets, soft and low.
Nature's stage, a playful tease,
Time to play, not just to grow.

With a wink, the twilight glows,
Wavy roads and silly hats.
Every splash, a ripple shows,
In this world of furry chats.

Chasing dreams, we skip and twirl,
As the dusk paints skies in blush.
Each moment, we unfurl,
In this vibrant, joyful rush.

Nature's Quiet Poetry

Raccoons writing rhymes at night,
Underneath the starry beams.
Bugs recite their buzzing sights,
In the quiet of our dreams.

Whispers in the gentle breeze,
Leaves exchanging scandal tales.
Hopping frogs take their ease,
While the cricket gently wails.

Squirrels gossip in their trees,
As they nibble nuts in peace.
Nature's laughter, light and free,
Sending worries to release.

In the stillness, giggles flow,
Each creature in its cozy nook.
Nature knows how to bestow,
Joy and life in every look.

Autumn's Heartbeat

Pumpkin spice, a cheeky grin,
Sweaters hug with warmth and cheer.
Footsteps crunching, let's begin,
To embrace the autumn near.

Goblins dance beneath the moon,
Costumed friends, a sight to see.
Laughter bubbles, joyous tune,
Every turn's a mystery.

Spirits roam with silly flair,
Sharing tales both bold and strange.
Each heartbeat bounces in the air,
As colors shift and lives exchange.

Gather round the crackling flames,
Ghostly whispers stir the night.
We'll relive our childhood names,
In this season, pure delight.

The Secrets of Stillness

In the hush where giggles hide,
Frogs strike poses, ready to play.
The moon looks down, with open eyes,
On these secrets of the day.

Rustling leaves, they hold their breath,
Telling tales of summer's end.
Every breeze has dance in depth,
Nature's smiles around the bend.

Whiskers twitch in grass so tall,
As creatures peek just for a peek.
Nature's antics, oh so small,
With laughter echoing, they speak.

In this quiet, joy awaits,
Every moment full of jest.
Life's a game, with simple fates,
Find the fun in every quest.

Twilight's Kaleidoscope

In twilight's glow, the leaves do twirl,
Squirrels dance, in a nutty swirl.
Chasing shadows, they leap and bounce,
Nature's jesters, in a leafy pounce.

A tip of hats to autumn's cheer,
Cadence of crunch, we can't endear.
The wind's a joker, whistling bright,
Rustling secrets under the night.

Colors clash like socks on a clown,
Golden yellows throwing the brown.
Every step, a comedic slip,
As the forest takes us on a trip.

In dusk's embrace, we laugh and play,
Nature's own cabaret, hooray!
With every leaf that tumbles down,
Our giggles echo, a joyful sound.

The Quiet Cradle of Leaves

Leaves hush softly, a cuddly bed,
Where dreams of acorns dance in red.
Chipmunks snicker, when no one's near,
Sharing tales of their autumn cheer.

A lazy fox in stripes of gold,
Tells jokes to trees both shy and old.
Funky fungi, like hats they wear,
In this cradle, nothing's a scare.

All the critters, a comedy troupe,
Gather 'round for the evening loop.
With every rustle, a giggle flows,
As nature's humor brightly glows.

Starlit skies and a moonbeam's wink,
Lead us to chuckle and think.
In this cradle, laughter is found,
Among the leaves, joy knows no bound.

Footsteps on Frosted Paths

Frosty mornings wrap the ground,
With every footstep, snickers abound.
Bouncing bunnies dance with glee,
While I slip sideways, oh woeful me!

Pinecones fall like comedic bombs,
Nature's way of sharing charms.
Squirrels giggle with acorn eyes,
As I pirouette, a dirk in disguise.

Frosty kisses on my nose,
Tickle my smile like candy prose.
Leaves freeze in fits of autumn play,
As laughter echoes, come what may.

In this chilly coat of white,
Nature's pranks are a pure delight.
With each crackle underfoot,
We stroll as jesters, absolute.

Against the Backdrop of Autumn's Fade

Leaves drop whispers from heights untold,
As jovial spirits begin to unfold.
The colors clash in a merry fight,
Orange and red, a comical sight.

Amidst the foliage, roly-poly folks,
Tell riddles and puns in silly strokes.
In this parade of crispy cheer,
Laughter rings clear, inviting all near.

The air is thick with giggly seeds,
As nature plays sways, a dance that leads.
To pumpkin patches and wild hayrides,
Where laughter abounds, and joy collides.

As days grow shorter and shadows play,
We dance through dusk, come what may.
In the fading hour, we won't retreat,
Laughter's sweet echo is our heartbeat.

A Harvest of Memories

In the orchard where apples bounce,
I tripped over my cheeky blouse.
Wobbling laughter fills the air,
As I dance without a care.

Silly squirrels eye my pie,
With their beady little spy.
I wave a spatula, dance real quick,
They chew my crust; oh, what a trick!

Sunbeams tickle the vibrant trees,
Who knew wind could tease like bees?
Chasing shadows, we twist and twirl,
Life is a whirl, give it a whirl!

As the harvest ends, we all agree,
Life's perfect with a fruit jubilee.
With friends beside and giggles spry,
We gather here, oh, me, oh my!

Embered Dreams

Under stars, we weave our tales,
Of misadventures, near misses, fails.
With marshmallows stuck in our hair,
We debate if the fire is 'rare.'

Just last night, I tried to roast,
A hotdog that turned into a toast.
We shrieked as it danced in the flames,
The hotdog's gone, but not our games!

Laughter echoed, wrapped in night,
Surely ghosts joined in our plight.
While shadows frolicked, dreams took flight,
In embered glow, all felt just right.

Chasing fireflies, we played tag,
One flew off with my snack bag.
You'll never guess how it all ended,
With dreams of food, oh how splendid!

The Symphonies of Surrender

One sunny day, we found a hat,
It's so big, we sat down flat.
Three of us tried to wear it right,
And ended up in a tangle fight!

With songs of squirrels serenading,
We skated on leaves, sideways parading.
Chasing dreams like chasing birds,
Yelling nonsense, just silly words.

We built a fort made of twigs and glee,
With fortunes told by a guessing bee.
Each riddle spun with laughter bright,
In this restroom of joy, what a sight!

As sun dips low, we bid adieu,
Not forgetting the laughter glue.
In our hearts, the symphony plays,
As memories dance through all our days.

Twilight in a Leafy Glade

In twilight's haze, the fireflies blink,
We ponder mysteries 'round the drink.
A leaf fell down, landed on my nose,
Oh, what a sight — everyone froze!

We shared tall tales with giggles loud,
Of wild animals and brave, proud.
A raccoon stopped by, cheeky and sly,
He snatched my snack and said goodbye!

With shadows creeping, we play charades,
Underneath the leafy glades.
Each pose we struck was pure delight,
And bats joined in; what a funny sight!

As stars appeared in brilliant spree,
We laughed until we couldn't see.
In the glade, legends were won,
As twilight danced, our hearts had fun!

A Canvas of Earthly Echoes

In the park, the squirrels play,
Chasing leaves that dance away.
With acorns flying here and there,
They seem to not possess a care.

Pigeon pals hold meetings near,
Plotting schemes from tree to sphere.
With every nut and crumb they find,
They're living life, unbound, unlined.

Resonate with Rustling Rhythms

The trees are chuckling, oh so sly,
As breezes whisper, "Give it a try!"
A leaf fell down, a graceful swoop,
Making jokes of the loyal troop.

A child runs past with sticky hands,
While candy wrappers mimic bands.
The rustling giggles make us grin,
Nature's laughter, where fun begins.

Leaves in the Lexicon of Time

Golden pages, time will tell,
A gust of wind, it's quite a spell.
As leaves swirl round like whirling dervish,
They tell stories, quite outlandish.

Napping beneath the great oak's shade,
Dreams take flight, adventures made.
With every fall, a tale is spun,
Time's library, where leaves have fun.

Glimmering with Golden Hues

Under sunlight, they seem to gleam,
Each leaf a character, part of a dream.
They chuckle as they bid goodbye,
Promising to return, oh my!

With every rustle, a laugh that's shared,
Nature's antics cannot be compared.
In this tapestry of red and gold,
Life's punchlines are sweetly told.

Hidden Steps Among the Fallen Pines

In the glen where mischief brews,
I tripped over a pile of shoes.
Those soft brown leaves, they slid and slipped,
Each step a giggle, each fall a quip.

Chipmunks watched with eyes so wide,
As I pranced like a clumsy guide.
The pines above all scratched their heads,
Wondering why I danced instead.

Squirrels laughed, they knew the score,
As I tangled with sticks, who needs a floor?
Nature's stage, in all its charm,
Providing laughter, and no harm.

With each slip, a tale I weave,
Autumn's jest, one can't believe.
In fallen pines, the humor reigns,
As my laughter mingles with the rains.

Portraits of Withering Branches

Once a tree with leaves so proud,
Now it wears its garb like a shroud.
"Cough up that twig!" the branches cried,
While passing birds just laughed and sighed.

One branch declared, "I've had enough,"
"Why must we look so worn and tough?"
The other snapped back with a scoff,
"Just wait till spring, we'll show them off!"

A squirrel painted smiles in the bark,
While pondering if he'd make his mark.
With every droop, there came a grin,
For in decay, the fun begins.

Each portrait tells a joke or two,
As nature dons a funner hue.
With every crack, a chuckle grows,
Amidst the withered, laughter flows.

The Soundtrack of Swaying Leaves

Rustling whispers in the breeze,
A symphony played with perfect ease.
Leaves chuckle as they dance and spin,
Creating tunes where fun begins.

"A little louder," one leaf cried,
"I'm drowning in this silly tide!"
The branches shook, they joined the song,
As nature's choir sang along.

The acorns dropped a rhythmic beat,
While squirrels tapped their tiny feet.
The melody, it swayed and soared,
Infected every soul aboard.

"Mistaken notes?" the birds did jest,
As if they knew just what was best.
Among the trees, the laughter weaves,
The joyful sounds of swaying leaves.

Tangled in Autumn Dreams

In a patchwork quilt of reds and golds,
Lies a tale that laughter holds.
"Oops, I'm stuck!" a raccoon shrieked,
Through tangleweed, a funny peeked.

The scarecrow winked with threads askew,
As if to say, "This joke's for you!"
With every twist, a chuckle grew,
In autumn's grasp, oh how they flew.

Dancing pumpkins filled with cheer,
Giggled loudly, "Let's persevere!"
A swirl of leaves, a dervish spree,
Nature joins this jolly jubilee.

As stars peek out to join the dream,
The night unfolds with laughter's scheme.
In tangled webs of autumn scenes,
We find the humor in our dreams.

The Dance of Amber Foliage

Gold leaves twirl in breezy spins,
Squirrels join the wild chagrins.
A gusty waltz, a frolic free,
Nature's giggles, can't you see?

Twisting in their autumn cheer,
They whisper secrets, oh so near.
Chasing shadows, they won't cease,
In this forest, life's a feast!

Feet slip on the golden ground,
Falling laughter all around.
A tree trunk gives a comic bow,
What fun with leaves, oh take a vow!

As raindrops fall, the color fades,
But still, they dance in leafy parades.
With every crunch beneath our toes,
A joyful jest that nature knows.

Echoes of Crimson Trails

Footprints left on scarlet beds,
Where squirrels dream with tiny heads.
They plot and scheme in sneak attack,
To steal a snack from your backpack!

Rustling whispers fill the air,
As leaves conspire without a care.
They plot an ambush—what a game!
To tickle toes, oh what a shame!

Each step you take, they crunch with glee,
A symphony of mischief, you see.
Fallen soldiers of autumn's reign,
Awakening the pranks, oh what a gain!

And as the sun dips low with flair,
The crimson carpet shows its wear.
But laughter lingers, floating high,
Echoes of joy as seasons fly.

Nostalgic Canopy

Beneath the trees, we reminisce,
In crinkled leaves, there's laughter's kiss.
A swing hung low from branches wide,
We climb, we swing, with youthful pride!

The canopy's a quilted dream,
Where time skips by in playful gleam.
With every flutter, memory springs,
A canvas lush where laughter sings.

The critters watch with knowing grins,
While we recall our youthful sins.
Each leaf a tale, a giggly plot,
In this bright world, we're still quite hot!

As shadows stretch and colors play,
We dance beneath, come what may.
This vibrant stage, this leafy host,
We celebrate what matters most.

Remnants of a Rustling Past

The crunch of leaves beneath our feet,
A symphony of autumn's beat.
We stumble through this kaleidoscope,
In twisted tales, we find our hope.

Old photographs of days gone by,
With goofy grins and painted sky.
A pumpkin's grin from long ago,
We laugh aloud, to not let go!

Faded colors, yet bright with mirth,
In every leaf, we find our worth.
Like giggling sprites on foliage trails,
Leaping softly, where laughter prevails!

So here's a toast to stories shared,
In rustling leaves and friendships spared.
In every turn, a sigh, a cheer,
We gather close, the end is near.

A Tapestry of Fallen Leaves

Once vibrant greens turned to squeaky yellows,
Squirrels plotting heists in the forests' meadows.
A dance of colors, so vibrant and bright,
Leaves whisper secrets, oh, what a delight!

The ground is a canvas, a slippery scene,
Where kids make a ruckus and jump like a bean.
Moms yell, 'No jumping!' but giggles abound,
As mud-covered sneakers are joyfully found.

Each stomp sends leaves swirling, a flurry of fun,
Like living confetti beneath autumn sun.
A critter parade, they scurry and jive,
Making a spectacle, oh, how they thrive!

At dusk, as the chill starts to creep and sneak,
The antics continue, a playful critique.
For nature's own circus, with laughter and cheer,
Turns even the grumpiest frowns to a smear.

The Embrace of Autumn Light

Soft golden rays filter through branches wide,
While pumpkins play dress-up, in fields they divide.
Frolicking friends in their knitted up gear,
Chasing after shadows, not thoughts of the year.

A squirrel in a hat, quite fashionably late,
Dances on branches, oh, isn't he great?
With acorns for bling and a tail like a king,
He prances around, making the whole forest sing.

The sun's a warm giggle, pulling you near,
While rakes turn to instruments of mirth and cheer.
With each leaf that tumbles, a new joke unfurls,
On this autumn stage, where laughter twirls.

As evening approaches, the jokes turn to screams,
With kids dashing home, clutching candy-filled dreams.
But the light leaves a promise, bright and delight,
That tomorrow will come, with laughter in sight.

Chaotic Beauty of Decay

The trees wear their gold like a dress full of flair,
While nature's own perfumist lingers in air.
A comedy of errors, oh, what a sight,
As leaves tumble down in a seasonal fight!

Fallen beauties decorate roads like art,
While children run wild, each fiend with a heart.
With swirls and with twirls, they kick through the ground,
Creating a symphony, joy all around.

Old Jack's gone and done it, his pie's more than sweet,
With spices and laughter, who can resist eat?
He guffaws in his kitchen, his recipe throne,
The neighbors all gather, it's quite the big show!

As shadows grow longer, the fun won't abate,
With stories of squirrels discussing their fate.
For even in chaos, there's beauty and play,
What a time to be silly, come join in the fray!

The Gold That Remains

In a heap of bright crunch, the laughter cascades,
As friends dive in leaf piles, in shimmering shades.
Like treasure hunters digging for joy all around,
Unearthing pure bliss with each rustling sound.

Jack-o'-lanterns grin, proud on every door,
While trick-or-treaters plot the next candy score.
With costumes like traffic cones, silly and loud,
They dash through the night, a festive, wild crowd.

The cider's all bubbling, a frothy delight,
While donuts, still warm, make each moan sound bright.
And stories of goblins, with glee they're retold,
As friendships grow deeper, like leaves made of gold.

As autumn winds whistle, tales waltz through the air,
With giggles, and laughter hanging everywhere.
A season of bounty, oh, how it entertains,
With joy wrapped in colors, forever remains.

Remnants of a Fading Season

The leaves are dancing, what a sight,
Taking turns in a comical flight.
Some land on dogs, others on heads,
Creating laughter wherever they tread.

Squirrels are plotting, oh what a tease,
Hoarding acorns like they're buying cheese.
They jump and tumble, a furry parade,
In this buffoonish charade, they're made.

A gust of wind sends hats to roam,
One lands on a neighbor, miles from home.
Children giggle, the playground's a show,
As nature provides the grandest tableau.

So gather 'round as the days grow cool,
Watch the antics, join in the fool.
In this season of chuckles, let's all partake,
For laughter's the treat that autumn will bake.

Echoes in the Underbrush

In the thickets, a rustle, what's that noise?
A chipmunk's stealing! Oh, such poise.
With a stash of seeds that makes him a lord,
He struts with pride, his tiny hoard.

The branches shake with a squirrel's sweet glee,
Dueling for nuts like it's reality TV.
One slips and tumbles, a clumsy ballet,
While friends all gather to laugh and play.

A hedgehog rolls by, in a prickly ball,
Thinking he's stealthy but he's got no gall.
Pine cones get tossed, a chuckling mess,
With every new tumble, we love him no less.

Amidst the ruckus, the laughter does swell,
Nature's own circus, it's magic, I tell!
In the underbrush, giggles take flight,
Echoes of autumn, a playful delight.

The Yearning of Gilded Leaves

Fallen leaves dance with a clumsy grace,
Rainbow confetti, a riotous place.
A leaf tried to swerve but landed on me,
Its twirling antics were quite the spree.

A tree shakes its branches, "It's time to let go!"
While the others whisper, "You're stealing the show!"
Each leaf has a story, a mishap or two,
As they flutter and flop, saying adieu.

Tripping on leaves is an art form, you see,
One step leads to laughter, particularly me.
As I tumble around, a giggling mess,
Autumn's a joker, I must confess.

So thank you, dear leaves, for the joy that you bring,
For a season of laughter, oh you clever thing!
Your yearning to fall, yet joyful in flight,
Turns an ordinary day into pure delight.

Portraits in the Breeze

Caught in the wind, a whimsical sight,
Leaves painting pictures, oh what a flight!
A leaf on a bike? Who thought that was grand?
And a dandelion drifting, an artist unplanned.

Clouds lend their canvas, brushing shades bright,
As butterflies dance in the warm golden light.
In this gallery, everyone's free,
To laugh at the chaos that nature can be.

A twig becomes famous, a budding star,
With fans made of petals that travel afar.
A scarecrow chuckles, his straw hat in glee,
While pumpkins roll by, as proud as can be.

So let's frame these moments, in laughter and jest,
In autumn's own portrait, we're all truly blessed.
As the breeze blows with mischief, it tickles our soul,
Rendering memories that make us feel whole.

Shades of Amber Reverie

Leaves waltz down with a playful sway,
Dancing around like they're in a play.
Squirrels hoard nuts with a frantic dash,
While the wind giggles in a leafy splash.

Pies cool on windows, tempting and bright,
Each slice a treasure, a pure delight.
But watch your step, oh, what a surprise!
A rogue acorn may cause a surprise!

The sun dips low, casting shadows long,
Critters sing out in a quirky song.
There's laughter and joy, in every nook,
As nature doles out her playful cook.

In this hour of amber cheer,
Bumbling bees buzz without fear.
Every twist, every turn, there's fun to unfold,
With tales of the past, lively and bold.

The Orchard's Farewell

The old tree creaks with tales untold,
Whispers of summers bright and bold.
Its fruits hang low, in layers of cheer,
But dodging them falling, oh dear, oh dear!

Gather 'round for cider, fresh and sweet,
The neighbors all come to take a seat.
With pies and laughter, the orchard is bright,
But one rogue apple gave a cheeky fright!

Baskets overflows with red and gold,
Yet some apples hang on stubborn and bold.
They claim pride, not ready to roll,
Declaring, "We're the stars of the stroll!"

As twilight descends, the branches sway,
As if they're bidding farewell to the day.
With a humor so rich and twists so grand,
The orchard sighs, "Take my hand!

Carved in Gnarled Bark

Names etched deep in gnarled embrace,
Love declared in this sacred space.
Teenage dreams in a playful tone,
With each carving, growth is shown.

Next to hearts, a squirrel stands proud,
Holding a nut, lost in the crowd.
Every scratch tells its own sweet tale,
Of those who loved and tried to prevail.

Tree rings speak of years gone by,
But whispers of laughter never die.
A splintered branch waves with a grin,
Echoes of joy wrapped tight within.

Beneath the canopy, memories blend,
Where every story has a twist to send.
Under the leaves, quirky tales arise,
In this forest, laughter never lies.

Stories on the Breeze

The wind rustles through the colorful leaves,
Spinning tales of long-lost eves.
Each gust carries laughter, drifting along,
With whispers of mischief, a joyful song.

Listen closely! There's a tale to share,
Of silly squirrels and a friendly bear.
Their antics leave us in fits of glee,
As they race through trees, wild and free.

A crow perched high, with cawing delight,
Tells jokes to the fox who's ready to bite.
But the fox just grins and winks an eye,
For who can resist? That's no reason to cry!

As twilight settles and stars appear,
Stories weave through the atmosphere.
With every chuckle carried on high,
The charm of nature makes spirits fly.

Fragments of Now and Then

In the garden of my youth,
A squirrel stole my sandwich,
With a flick of bushy tail,
Off he went, oh what a bandit!

Old photos faded, turning gray,
Grandma danced in her polka dots,
Her laugh echoing from the past,
As grandpa tried to pop the corn!

A kite stuck high in the tree,
We dared not climb to get it down,
An epic battle with the wind,
Victory tasted like cotton candy.

Now I miss those silly days,
With laughter woven through the air,
Time flies like a silly goose,
Yet the mischief never fades!

Twilight's Embrace

The sun dips low, a golden glow,
Fireflies start their tiny show,
I trip over my own two feet,
Belly laughs as the grass feels sweet.

In that twilight, the frogs all sing,
Their croaks compete with crickets' cling,
As shadows dance upon the lawn,
I swear that tree is just a con!

A barbecue gone slightly wrong,
First we burned the buns, so long!
Pulled out the grill, but it's a mess,
Dinner served with humor, not stress.

Days are silly, nights are bright,
In twilight's embrace, we take flight,
With every giggle, we proclaim,
Life's perfect blend of joy, not fame!

Autumn's Whisper

Leaves are falling, like confetti,
Sweater weather, feeling heady,
Jack-o'-lanterns grin with fright,
As ghosts sneak up to share the night.

A dance with leaves, they swirl and twirl,
I trip and fall, give them a whirl,
The yard's a mess, a crunchy play,
With laughter echoing, bright and gay.

Hot cocoa spills, oh dear, oh no!
Marshmallows floating, quite the show,
But we all sip and giggle wide,
Autumn whispers, "Just enjoy the ride!"

As the days shorten, we stay close,
Gather stories, laugh the most,
Autumn brings its funny cheer,
In whimsical moments, we hold dear!

Golden Leaves of Memory

In a pile of leaves, we dive right in,
Making forts where fun can begin,
Each rustle hides a secret laugh,
As playful winds join the gaffe.

Skipping rocks and silly squawks,
A squirrel judges from the docks,
His acorns hoarded, quite a stash,
While we take turns in a leaf splash.

Hot cider spills on our warm clothes,
Laughter erupts, a cheerful prose,
With each sweet sip, tales unfold,
Of silly things that never get old.

Golden leaves brighten our hearts,
In time, we learn it's just the start,
With joy in each whimsical twist,
These golden days are not to miss!

Weaving Warmth into October

In October's gentle chill, I wear my turtleneck,
Remembering the time I tripped on a dog's trek.
The leaves conspire, whispering in my ear,
'Embrace the season; it's not time to veer.'

I brew a drink to stave the cold retreat,
Oh, how I danced around the cat's swift feet!
Pumpkin spice, my stomach's battle cry,
As squirrels invade my stash; oh my, oh my!

The scarves and hats, an odd ensemble they form,
Fashion statements made that break the norm.
But hey, it's October, let the laughter reign,
While nature pulls its quirks; we can't complain!

So here's to warm moments, a chuckle or two,
As leaves and giggles swirl in vibrant hue.
With sweaters knotted tight and cocoa sipped slow,
We'll weave these tales together, let the crisp winds blow!

A Journey Through the Canopy

On a quest up high, I swung from a branch,
Only to find out it's not a good stance.
The leaves all laughed; I waved them goodbye,
As the ground rushed up; oh my, oh my!

Birds chirped their gossip; I caught their decree,
'Watch out for squirrels; they're plotting, you see!'
I tiptoed along, in my brightest red shoes,
Wondering which path would end up in blues.

A friendly raccoon gave directions with flair,
But he forgot to mention—beware of the bear!
I dashed past the bushes, heart racing like mad,
Who knew a climb could result in such bad?

In the end, I giggled and thanked my feet,
For every mishap makes the journey sweet.
With leaves swirling down like confetti in air,
I'll cherish this trek, my whimsical dare!

Rooted in Autumn's Embrace

With roots deep in laughter, I bask in the glow,
Of stories from past that seem to overflow.
My grandma's old sweater, too big and too bright,
Made me the fashionista of every Halloween night!

I try to dance, but the leaves drop their bets,
They twirl and they fall, and I'm stuck with the pets.
The dog leaps and bounds, while I tumble and roll,
But laughter is stitched in autumn's warm soul.

The napping cats plot my next fashion faux pas,
While I sip cider and survey from afar.
The sun dips low, and I zone out with glee,
Autumn's embrace feels just like a big hug from me.

So here's to the moments, a riotous blend,
Of folly and fun, where giggles ascend.
Roots running deep in this cozy tableau,
With laughter and warmth, let the good times flow!

Shadows on a Painted Path

On this painted path, I stroll with a bounce,
Tangled up in laughter—I'm lost, but who's to announce?

The shadows dance funny, play tricks on my feet,
As pumpkins stare wide-eyed, they're wanting a treat!

Fallen leaves chatter, like gossiping friends,
'Watch out for that squirrel; let the chaos commence!'
I stumble on acorns; my balance is fleeting,
But who can stay serious while autumn's still greeting?

Each footstep a giggle, each moment a glee,
As shadows keep shifting, they're playing with me.
Hoping I'm wiser as the paths twist and twine,
Just chasing the daylight, where laughter blurs the line.

So let's paint this path with stories and chuckles,
Where shadows play tricks and silliness snuggles.
In the heart of this season, let whimsy declare,
That laughter will echo through crisp autumn air!

The Leaf-Note Letters

In the breeze, the letters fly,
Whispering secrets from trees up high.
A squirrel's giggle, a funny chase,
Leaves dance around in a comical race.

Each note's a jest, a pun in disguise,
An acorn's wisdom, it surely supplies.
With ink of sap, the stories unfold,
Of chipmunk pranks and a heart full of gold.

Crinkled pages, like fabric worn,
From the tales of laughter, a friendship is born.
A raccoon's riddle, a turtle's pun,
Under the sun, the fun's never done.

Oh, the joy of a leaf's silly flight,
In the autumn's glow, such pure delight.
So gather 'round, share a tale or two,
In the laughter of leaves, old friendships renew.

Stories Beneath the Canopy

Under the boughs where the squirrels play,
Tales are told in a jumbled way.
A robin sings a tune out loud,
While dandelion wishes float through the crowd.

The owl hoots jokes from the old oak's side,
With wise-cracking wisdom, he takes pride.
"Why did the leaf refuse to fall?
It didn't want to end up in a ball!"

A gust of wind brings giggles to all,
A jester's trick that's hard to recall.
The raccoon juggles nuts with flair,
While the chipmunks cheer, "That's beyond compare!"

So join the fun, don't miss the show,
Beneath the trees where the laughter does grow.
Each crack of a branch, a laugh or two,
In the stories below, there's joy for you!

Shades of September Reflections

In September's hue, the jokes take flight,
Leaves share haikus and giggle at night.
A funny filter on the woods so grand,
As shadows dance in a playful band.

"Why did the tree start to sing?"
"My roots feel great, I'm the queen of spring!"
A chorus of chuckles beneath the sun,
With every leaf rustle, the fun has begun.

As the sun sets low, the colors collide,
A cartoonish sunset, a joyride slide.
Throughout the forest, let the humor reign,
In shades of laughter, none feel the strain.

So take a stroll beneath this display,
Where laughter lingers at the end of day.
Each shade reflects, a smile in bloom,
In the funny light, there's a playful room.

Harvest of Warmth

In the season of harvest, what do we find?
Pumpkin spice nonsense, all intertwined.
Acorns are gathered, but with a twist,
Squirrels in capes, they can't be missed.

A basket of giggles, that's what we need,
Fruits of the season, a laughter seed.
"Why did the pumpkin sit all alone?
It saw all the squash and just wouldn't moan!"

Under the bounty, hilarity blooms,
With apples that dance and dance floors of plumes.
A corn maze mystery, no map in sight,
But silly scarecrows help us find light.

So let's raise a toast to the autumn's delight,
With warmth in our hearts, and laughter in sight.
In each byte of harvest, we find cozy cheer,
With funny tales shared, the season is clear.

Dancing With the Wind

Leaves wiggle on the trees,
Chasing breezes with such ease.
Whispers giggle, branches bend,
Nature's dance, no need to pretend.

Squirrels twirl in grand display,
Dressed in fur, they leap and sway.
A leaf pirouettes in flight,
What a show on autumn's night!

Down the path they twirl and sway,
Casting shadows, come what may.
The world's a stage, as they twine,
Who knew leaves could toe the line?

With every gust, a chuckle shared,
In this leafy ball, none are scared.
So join the fun, let worries cease,
As foliage throws a wild feast!

Threads of a Leafy Legacy

Once there lived a leaf so bold,
Crafted tales yet to be told.
Each thread spun with laughs and glee,
A woven tale of leaf and tree.

In the wind, it played a tune,
Bouncing high, a little moon.
The bark chortled, swaying low,
"That funny leaf, the star of the show!"

With acorns falling, squirrels pranced,
Around it, all the critters danced.
It shouted jokes to the resting stones,
Echoes mingled, in cheerful tones.

And though it faded with the fall,
Its laughter lingered, bright and tall.
Memories spun, like threads of yarn,
Tales of joy in every barn!

Remembrance in Red and Gold

Crisp air wraps in colors bold,
Giggles scattered, tales retold.
The maples blush in firelight,
As creatures waddle with delight.

Down the lane, a leaf parade,
Flaunting hues that never fade.
Silly squirrels in their stash,
Forget their worries in a flash!

Fallen leaves share secrets old,
Of summers past, of winter cold.
Each crunch beneath a footstep's sway,
Brings laughter back, come what may!

Through every rustle, jokes take flight,
As nature's punchlines feel just right.
So toast the gold, the red and brown,
To memories that never drown!

Twilight of the Canopy

As sunlight fades, the shadows play,
Leaves chatter as if to say,
"Is it bedtime for us tonight?
Or shall we dance in fading light?"

The owls hoot with bemused grin,
As the branches twist and spin.
Creatures nibble on fading snacks,
Underneath the leafy tracks.

Swaying gently, whispers blend,
With gossip that will never end.
The canopy, a playful host,
Holds laughter close as we all boast!

With a final flutter, night descends,
A jolly time that never bends.
In twilight's embrace, we all proclaim,
"Nature's jokes put us to shame!"

Seasons of Love in Flushed Hues

In twilight's glow, we dance with glee,
Each step a crunch, oh what a spree!
We dress in colors, bright and bold,
And laugh about our starts as old.

With every swirl, the laughter flows,
A slip, a spin, oh how it shows!
We prance like kids, so carefree still,
And gather leaves, that's quite a thrill!

The air is crisp, our cheeks are red,
The tales of love are sweetly said.
With pockets full of nature's gold,
We spread our joy, a sight to behold!

In cozy nooks, the stories brew,
Of wild escapades both tried and true.
With flustered hearts, we eat our pie,
As leaves fall softly from the sky.

Flickering Memories of a Leafy Past

In a world of yellow, red and brown,
We twirl like clowns, never a frown.
The squirrels giggle with acorn treats,
While we recount our summer feats.

From teeny top hats made of bark,
To coffee stained knees, what a lark!
With whispers of wind, we twist and roam,
Chasing our shadows, finding our home.

A game of tag 'neath branches wide,
With laughter spilling like a tide.
Each memory brighter than the last,
As we celebrate this leafy past.

In curls of steam from cups we sip,
We find delight in every trip.
With friends around, life's a cheer,
These flickering moments, dear and clear.

Wandering Beneath the Golden Canopy

Underneath the shimmering bright,
We wander on, hearts feeling light.
A dance of rays through branches peek,
With every rustle, secrets speak.

Our laughter echoes, a silly song,
With each funny step, we can't go wrong.
We banter on about autumn's charm,
And dodge the branches that mean us harm.

Caught in a tangle of twirling leaves,
We stumble, tumble, no one believes!
With giggles rising to the sky,
Who knew these leaves could make us fly?

Wrapped in colors of amber hue,
We sit and share dreams, both old and new.
As the sun sets and shadows play,
Wandering still, we miss the day!

Threads of Cinnamon and Copper

With threads of gold and copper sheen,
We weave our tales, both fun and keen.
In the garden where mischief blooms,
We giggle, tasting sweet perfumes.

The pumpkin patch holds tales of yore,
Where we once tripped, then laughed some more.
With cinnamon spice in every bite,
Our memories dance in pure delight.

Through tangled vines and funky hats,
We flash our smiles with silly chats.
As leaves fall gently, so do our woes,
In threads of laughter, anything goes!

And with each sip of apple brew,
We toast to moments that flew and flew.
In cozy corners, our hearts align,
Sharing the joy of all that is divine.

Crimson Cascade

In the brisk air, we dance around,
Dodging leaves that tumble down,
A cascade of colors, bright and bold,
Nature's way of being uncontrolled.

Squirrels plot as they stash their treats,
With tiny paws and hasty beats,
One leaps too high and takes a dive,
Land on a pile, oh, how they thrive!

Pumpkin spice in every cup,
Watch for latte spills, hold up!
Friends burst into laughter and cheer,
As whipped cream flies, oh dear!

So here's to the autumn's playful show,
With every crunch, it's fun to go,
In the fall breeze, life's a blast,
Making memories, oh, how they last!

Autumn's Whispered Secrets

The trees gossip in quiet tones,
Branches twist like silly bones,
Whispers of squirrels in clever schemes,
Plotting heists of acorn dreams.

Golden leaves wear fancy hats,
While birds argue about their spats,
Who eats more worms, the blue or red?
Round and round, their debates spread.

Pies are baked with spice so sweet,
But losing weight is quite the feat,
Apple cider spills, not a care,
Just giggles float up in the air.

As jackets rustle and children dart,
Falling leaves act like works of art,
The canvas beneath, a raucous scene,
Whimsy reigns where joy has been.

Leaves of Lament

Oh, the plight of fallen leaves,
Sighing softly on autumn eves,
Once so proud upon the tree,
Now they lie and long to be free.

In piles they dream of flights once taken,
Of windy days, now forsaken,
Children jump with gleeful shouts,
While leaves grumble with tiny pouts.

Rakes in hand, the battle cries,
"Not my leaves!" an elderly sighs,
But laughter paints this canvas bright,
As friends create a joyful sight.

So let them lay, in peace, at last,
Their stories woven, memories amassed,
For every crunch that echoes clear,
Is proof of past fun, look and cheer!

The Tapestry of Fall

Stitches of orange, gold, and brown,
Crafting outfits for the town,
Sweaters too snug, but oh, the flair,
We shimmy and shake without a care.

Crisp air tickles, we blush and grin,
As we huddle close, we all fit in,
While bakeries flaunt their flaky treats,
With pumpkin flavors that can't be beat.

The dance of harvest, the clumsy art,
Corn mazes twist through every heart,
Lost and found in fields of corn,
Squeals erupt with each scare born.

Meeting friends, tales spun anew,
Of furry hats and things to do,
In this vibrant quilt of laughter's call,
Together we weave the tapestry of fall.

Treasures Tucked in the Treetops

Squirrels hoard nuts like it's a sport,
Planning their feasts, making a report.
Jackets of fur, their tails in a twist,
On branches so high, they coexist.

Ripe acorns roll, a game of chance,
Watch out below! It's the nutty dance.
With a cheeky grin, they leap and they prance,
While birds chirp away, giving them a glance.

Leaves rustle secrets, ripe with delight,
As critters conspire deep into the night.
Maples listen close to the tales they spin,
Of treasures and tricks, and mischief within.

So join in the fun in this leafy retreat,
With laughter and joy, on this treehouse seat.
The world is a buffet, oh what a treat,
Where treasures abound, and nothing's discreet.

The Map of Windy Roads

Take a wrong turn, find a tree in the way,
Oh look, there's a frog, what a curious display!
With roads that loop like a roller coaster,
We giggle and laugh, like a merry poster.

Potholes hide treasures, or so we assume,
The bumpy ride adds to the fun we consume.
GPS lost, but hey, who needs advice?
We'll trust the winds, perhaps roll the dice.

Rivers twist like spaghetti, how absurd!
Each bend shows laughter, it's totally unheard.
A wrong turn taken leads us to delight,
Where giggles echo beneath the moonlight.

So here's to the maps with their windy charm,
They often lead us to laughter, not harm.
Our journeys become tales of whimsy and cheer,
Navigating nonsense is what we hold dear.

Rust and Reverie

In scenes of gold, with crunches galore,
We stumble and slip, what a clumsy chore!
With leaves like confetti, we dance and we spin,
Creating our joy, as the laughter begins.

Old benches creaking, they've stories to tell,
Of lovers and misfits, under their spell.
We sit and reflect, with snacks on our lap,
Finding humor in time, it's a blissful trap.

A squirrel pops by with a cheeky little grin,
Stealing our crumbs, it's utter chagrin.
Yet we can't help but break into a laugh,
At this sneaky raccoon's daring new path.

So let's raise a toast to the rust of the fall,
To moments that make us feel big and small.
In every mishap, in each funny fall,
There's a spark of delight for us all.

Coated in Autumn's Glow

When jackets come out, and leaves start to drop,
We gather 'round fires, while the skies pop.
With marshmallows toasted, we chuckle and sneer,
For sticky-handed jokes, we hold so dear.

A leaf lands on heads like a quirky hat,
Oh the tales we'll tell of that sneaky spat.
With laughter like fireworks, bright in the night,
We cherish such moments, it's pure delight.

Hot cocoa spills, oh what a fine mess,
Here comes the giggles, we can't help but stress.
In their cozy embrace, we share our good cheer,
Who knew autumn's touch would bring forth such year?

So here's to the moments, both funny and bright,
In every warm hug, and warm firelight.
We'll treasure them all, in this season's flow,
With hearts that are full, and faces aglow.

Rustling Thoughts of Days Gone By

In the attic, I found some hats,
One looked like it belonged to a cat!
With polka dots and splashes of red,
I swear it whispered; 'Take me instead!'

Old photographs trapped in a roll,
With my hairdo that rivaled a troll.
I laugh at the styles of yesteryear,
Wish I could tell that girl, 'Never fear!'

Forgotten toys stacked high on a shelf,
That squeaked and creaked with a life of their own.
I mockingly named one 'Uncle Elf,'
As it danced on the breeze, all alone!

The old radio crackled with tunes,
Singing of love under bright, glowing moons.
I joined in, off-key, still feeling so spry,
With my socks mismatched to the world's high sigh!

The Window to Rustic Yesterdays

Peering through glass, the past calls me near,
With stories of mischief and jars of beer.
There's a squirrel that swore he could fly,
Till he landed in mud – oh my, oh my!

The porch swing creaked like an old rusty gate,
As I shared my schemes with my overgrown mate.
We plotted to catch fireflies bold,
But ended up tangled in ribbons of gold.

A runaway kite met a tree with a thud,
And our plans for the summer went down in a flood.
Yet I'll always recall those silly little things,
Like the joy of bad singing and how laughter rings!

Old boots and a bike, we rode 'til the sunset,
With friends that I promised I'd never forget.
Each memory woven in laughter and cheer,
Are treasures that linger, forever so dear.

Treasures in Crimson Shadows

In the garden, we found the oddest of things,
A shoe, half a mannequin, and rubber bands with strings.
We made up stories of where they could roam,
Imagining they had been far from home.

While searching for gold in the rustling leaves,
We stumbled upon our old dance of thieves.
With leaves stuck in our hair, we broke into song,
Claiming that we'd dance all night long!

A picnic blanket spread on the ground,
With sandwiches shaped like the crumpled sound.
We laughed as we nibbled, with crumbs in our beards,
And shared all our secrets, forgetting our fears.

The swing set creaked—it knew all our tales,
As we swung through the twilight, our laughter on trails.
Reminding us always, as days turned to night,
That fun waits for those who still find delight.

Echoes of Changing Seasons

The wind howled a tune in the orange-lit sky,
As we dressed up our dog with a hat way too high.
He shook it off proudly, 'No way, José!'
While we rolled on the ground, giggling all day.

Leaves twirled like dancers, our feet were a blur,
Chasing the shadows we'd happily stir.
I lost my shoe, and so did my friend,
'Two peas in a pod!' we'd chant till the end.

Snowflakes were falling, a fluffy white hug,
We built a snowman that looked like a bug!
A carrot for a nose that we snatched from the stew,
While the world around shimmered with joy that was new.

Those seasons of laughter, the echoes remain,
In the heart of our memories, joy we had gained.
Through sun, snow, and all of the rain,
We found in our folly, life's sweetest refrain.

The Soil of Forgotten Trails

Once I tripped on a fallen leaf,
And landed right by a silly thief.
He stole my sandwich, cheese and all,
While laughing at my belly's call.

We wandered paths, with snacks galore,
But who knew trails could have a score?
With every step, a crunch, a crack,
We chased the squirrels, they did not slack.

Under trees where shadows danced,
I thought I saw a bug romance.
It turned out to be a twig, not true,
Just my luck—what a fine to view!

As daylight fled and stars took flight,
We made a camp, all felt so right.
But fireflies glowed and then went poof,
Now where's my sandwich? Come on, hoof!

Eloquent Autumn Elegies

Oh, the leaves waltz down like crazy folks,
Spinning around in their funny cloaks.
One landed plop on a dog named Max,
He jumped so high, it broke the fax!

"Why wear a coat when you can shine?"
Said the tree to the squirrel sipping pine.
The squirrel rolled eyes—his snack was grand,
While I watched, munching chips, quite unplanned.

Each gust of wind plays a little prank,
On hesitant souls at the old bank.
I waved to a guy, thought he was a friend,
But it was a tree—today just won't end!

The sun sets low, and what do I see?
A raccoon wearing my hat with glee.
"Hey buddy, no stealing my autumn cheer!"
But he just grinned and had no fear!

Tales Written in the Wind

The breeze whispers tales of good times shared,
Of borrowed hats and how they fared.
One hat flew up with such great flair,
It landed on a scarecrow's hair!

We danced with clouds and chased a kite,
A game of tag in golden light.
But oh! The kite did take a dive,
Right into the soup where ants thrive!

"Oh what a mess!" I giggled loud,
As ants marched on—oh they are proud.
We laughed and splashed, as leaves took flight,
In a whirlwind of autumn's delight.

At sunset glow, we rolled on grass,
With stories that make this moment last.
When the wind tickles me just right,
I swear it tells jokes all through the night!

A Glimpse of Autumn's Essence

I spotted a pumpkin with a goofy grin,
It rolled away as I tried to win.
Chasing it down through the crunchy leaves,
The laughter spilled out in pleasant heaves.

Then came a cat—oh what's her game?
Pouncing on leaves, she thought it was fame.
A chase ensued, round and round we spun,
What a silly mishap; oh, autumn's fun!

Each passing moment, a chuckle shared,
With dancing critters who simply dared.
The air was crisp, the colors bright,
Who knew laughter could take such flight?

As evening fell, with stars above,
The memories layered like hand-knit glove.
In this charming chaos, joy's essence lies,
Autumn's a joke that never dies!

A Symphony in Rust and Gold

Crunching leaves beneath our shoes,
Each step a note in playful hues.
A squirrel dances with such flair,
While we just stand and gasp for air.

The breeze plays tricks, a playful tease,
As hats go flying with the breeze.
The trees chuckle, their laughter bold,
In this concert of rust and gold.

Autumn's laughter rings so free,
With acorns dropping from the tree.
A symphony of fun unfolds,
As we embrace the autumn gold.

In this season, joy's the goal,
Let's savor each sweet, crunchy roll.
With silly smiles and hearts so light,
We dance beneath this warm delight.

Journey Under the Amber Canopy

We set off with our picnic gear,
Beneath a sky so bright and clear.
But ants have plans for my potato,
They plot like tiny overlords, I say so!

Wobbly branches catch my hat,
As I hear a thump—what was that?
An acorn lands right on my head,
Now my hair's a nest instead!

We laugh at how we barely steer,
As leaves swirl down like confetti here.
Navigating fun with blissful glee,
In this amber kingdom, wild and free.

With snacks and giggles, oh, what a day,
It's a quirky journey, come what may.
Under the trees, a merry band,
Making memories, so planned and unplanned.

The Chorus of Autumn Gentlemen

The trees bow low, their coats so grand,
With sunlight dancing, a sparkling band.
The squirrels in tails, they take their stance,
As they join in for an autumn dance.

We tip our hats with jovial pride,
To the rustling leaves that swirl beside.
Each gust of wind, a cheeky prank,
That sends our voices up the plank.

The gentlemen of fall make quite a show,
With a chorus that makes spirits glow.
Laughing and singing, they spin around,
With each little leaf, fun's truly found.

A playful breeze, a round of cheer,
In golden hues, we shed a tear.
For these moments bright and moments bold,
With autumn's laughter, never cold.

Reminiscing the Hairpin Turns

We brave the trails that twist and wind,
With curves that leave our senses blind.
Each pothole offers a hearty laugh,
As we're jolted left, then down the path.

Among the pines, we spin and whirl,
Our heads a mess, each hair a swirl.
A leaf-strewn path, a bumpy ride,
With laughter bursting from inside.

A raccoon waves from a lofty perch,
We lose a shoe—what a funny search!
Each hairpin turn's a memory made,
As we conquer fall's grand parade.

So here's to leaves that catch our breath,
To silly moments we won't forget.
Through twists and turns, we find our way,
In laughter's light, we choose to stay.

www.ingramcontent.com/pod-product-compliance
Lightning Source LLC
Chambersburg PA
CBHW071849160426
43209CB00003B/477